WAR AND THE GREAT THRONE

JACOB ABSHIRE

War and the Great Throne
© 2015 by Jacob Abshire

Published by Truth411 and Lucid Books
18906 Par Two Cir., Humble, TX 77346
www.t411.com

Design and typeset: Resolute Creative, Inc., Houston, TX

WAR AND THE
GREAT THRONE

A STUDY GUIDE ABOUT
THE BATTLES FOR YOUR HEART

t411.com

Truth411
HOUSTON, TX

LUCIDBOOKS

CONTENTS

BEFORE YOUR JOURNEY

"You shall not pass!" My hands clutched a broom stick above my head and my eyes looked before me with the gravity of Gandalf. I stood between my twelve year old daughter and her bedroom. It was the perfect bonding moment. Instead of rolling her eyes and uttering some sarcastic remark like the rest of the world's pre-teen female species, she joined me in my brief departure from real life.

Her part was in slow motion. She reached out with one hand to grab me. Her other hand raised above her head to shield the arrows being launched in her direction. "Nooooo!" She stretched out as long as her inner wind would allow. I'm now in slow motion as well. I slammed the broom to the ground unleashing a sonic boom throughout the house. The tile floor shook and lightning flashed nearly blinding the both of us. My long gray robe swung into the air like a tornado was lifting it. The fiery pit below us smoldered with heat and hoisted embers upward. Then, it circled around us like a sparkling stronghold. You would have to see it to believe it.

"Um, what are ya'll doing?" Galadriel, I mean my wife, paused at the foot of the hallway. She stood there staring at us with her head tilted and brows squished together at the center of her temple. My daughter and I froze still. The movie was on pause. I looked at her. She looked at me. Then, we both looked at the elf down the hall—still frozen. The lady shook her head and turned toward another room as if to enter it, but stopped short. Leaning back into the hall, she looked one last time. Something caught her eye. It drew her in. She walked right up to me. What was she going to do? What evil was she going to unleash? "Huh," she said while grabbing the broom from my hand, "I've been looking for that." And, she walked away in the night.

Honestly, it was way more awesome than it sounds. Despite what you might think, there is no real moral to the story. I wanted to stop you for a moment and lock your imagination in for the context of this study guide. You will need it. So, in the spirit of imaginary stories, "You shall not pass!" At least, not until you know what we are doing with this little book. Here it is in a nutshell.

The Bible uses the word "heart" to describe the inner you—the critical part of your existence, the part that lives forever. It is where your intellect and will shake hands, make friends and make moves. It is the part of you that is you. It the seat of your soul. And, it is exactly what we are discussing in this series. The "throne" is used metaphorically to refer to your heart. And, pressing the metaphor further, we will bring in some elements of medieval war that serves as illustrations of our fight against sin, the sufferings we endure, the weapons of war, and the people who support and hold us up in battle.

Each chapter, including the introduction and closing, tells as complete story with you as the main actor. For this reason, it is best for you to read each in order. The introduction will set the stage for the story. The lessons carry you along the story plot-by-plot. And finally, the story comes to an end with a summary in the closing chapter.

So journey through the story of the *War and the Great Throne*. Get caught up in the story and most importantly, let the King, who has established His throne in the heavens, search your heart and help you wage your war against the enemy of your soul.

INTRODUCTION
THE RIGHTFUL KING

JESUS CHRIST IS THE BLESSED
AND ONLY SOVEREIGN, THE
KING OF KINGS AND LORD OF
LORDS, WHO ALONE HAS
IMMORTALITY, WHO DWELLS
IN UNAPPROACHABLE LIGHT.

— 1 TIMOTHY 6:15-16 —

THE STORY BEGINS

A sudden jolt of urgency pierces your heart and awakens you from sleep. Your heart is rejuvenated and beating more strongly, more resiliently. Inside, you feel resolved and renewed. But this renewal gives rise to a grave disturbance.

In your heart, you wonder where you have been all this time and what has happened while you slept. You arise and move toward the window, only to recognize things are not as you dreamed. The fields are grey as if burned to ash. The trees are bare. The livestock is feeble and sickly. The people are weak and ill. The kingdom you once stewarded is lifeless and decayed!

You see it for the first time. Your breathing deepens. Your heart skips. A deep voice whisks across your ears and is heard in the caverns of your soul. The utterance infuses you with clarity and a spirited sense of desperation. Things are not as they should be. While you were sleeping, another ruled your kingdom—a hopelessly wicked ruler.

Unfortunately, you don't have the power to change this desolation. Only one who is more powerful and more perfect in wisdom can restore the kingdom to its intended state.

The voice speaks to you of such a ruler. His wisdom is beyond the wisest in the land. His power exceeds all known sources of strength, even that of nature. He is the mightiest Sovereign, the King of all kings, and the lawful ruler of your kingdom. They call him the Rightful King.

LESSON ONE

THE GREAT THRONE

I WILL GIVE THEM A HEART TO KNOW THAT I AM THE LORD, AND THEY SHALL BE MY PEOPLE AND I WILL BE THEIR GOD, FOR THEY SHALL RETURN TO ME WITH THEIR WHOLE HEART.

— JEREMIAH 24:7 —

THE STORY CONTINUES

Beyond solemn castle walls lies a chamber so grave, only the finest guards in the kingdom stand before its gate. Positioned inside is the Great Throne where the king rules and loyalties reside. It is the heart of the kingdom.

But each hour, the violent clashing of wood and metal can be heard. It is the racket of war. Raging fiercely, the noise echoes throughout the halls and the mountainside. The shouts of menacing men stir unrest in all who hear. The battles never end.

The heart of the kingdom is most treasured. Kings from every countryside mount up to invade the halls and lay hold of the chamber. For whoever sits on the Great Throne rules the kingdom.

OPENING THOUGHTS

1. Why do you think the one who sits on the throne rules the kingdom? How is this possible? Does this happen today, maybe in different terms?

2. We don't live in a society like the times of thrones long ago, but we do live in an era where the same things happen—even at a personal level. How does this narrative relate to your life?

SEEING THE GREAT THRONE

The heart is the center of our body. It pumps life to every part of the body and maintains proper circulation of minerals and medicines. It beats an average of 75 times per minute—forty million times a year—discharging three thousand gallons of blood each day. In one hour, the heart does enough work to lift a grown man up a three-story building. It is a hard-working marvel!

In the Bible, the heart is used to describe the center of all things. When the proverb tells us to "trust in the Lord with all our heart," it means to give all your love and loyalty to God (Prov. 3:5). If your center trusts in the Lord, then the rest of you will, too. The heart is the Great Throne of your life. Whatever rules your heart rules your body.

3. How does something or someone rule you by ruling your heart? What are some examples?

4. What or who rules your heart right now? If you could see what kind of "life" is pumping through your body, what would it be?

5. How do you suppose the ruler of your heart rules your day? In other words, how does your heart tell you what you ought to do?

SURRENDERING THE GREAT THRONE

It is important that we know who rules our heart. By nature, we are called "children of wrath" because we are born with hearts that hate God's rule (Eph. 2:3). In fact, our hearts are so horrible, they even deceive themselves just to spite God (Jer. 17:9). What we need as sinners is not new arms and legs, but new hearts.

Jesus said only the "pure in heart will see God" (Matt. 5:8). This is a problem since we are born with impure hearts. The good news is that God can give us new hearts, and it is as simple as surrendering the Great Throne to Jesus (Jer. 24:7; Eph. 3:17). Tell your guards to stand aside and raise the white flag!

6. Since the king of your heart is the ruler of your life, how important is it to you to have the right King seated on the Great Throne? Why?

7. How do you suppose life would be different with another king on the throne? Why?

8. What has this lesson helped you realize? What decisions will you make today? What changes need to occur in your life?

CONCLUSION

The Great Throne needs a new king. The reigning king of our nature is desperately wicked and despises God. He prevents us from ultimately seeing God (Matt. 5:8). This is why we must surrender the throne to Jesus. We must allow Him to conquer the castle and sit on the seat of rule. Only He can give us a new heart with new love and loyalty. If Jesus is not your king, surrender your kingdom to Him now.

LESSON TWO

THE GOOD WAR

FIGHT THE GOOD FIGHT OF
THE FAITH. TAKE HOLD OF
THE ETERNAL LIFE TO WHICH
YOU WERE CALLED AND ABOUT
WHICH YOU MADE THE GOOD
CONFESSION IN THE
PRESENCE OF MANY
WITNESSES.

— 1 TIMOTHY 6:12 —

THE STORY CONTINUES

With the Rightful King on the throne, the stakes are highest and the war is fought more fiercely. Wannabe kings burn with greed. Their appetite for power is relentless. They will stop at nothing to lay hold of the Great Throne.

They march back and forth just outside the chamber courts and beyond the stone walls. You can hear them breathing with envy, pounding their chests and stomping their feet. The smallest of them bleed for war. The largest grunt for blood.

Each hour of each day, their trumpets sound forth a battle cry. Waves of envious hordes rush against the castle gates, pressing toward the throne they so madly desire. War is again unleashed, and the King's mighty men rush to battle. The blast of horns is drowned out by the cracking of bones and agony of pain. The Good War is being fought!

OPENING THOUGHTS

1. Why do you think the false kings wage war so fiercely to gain access to the Great Throne? What are they seeking to accomplish?

2. This is a picture of what is happening within us and, in another sense, around us. How does this narrative resemble the war of faith?

ENGAGING THE GOOD WAR

God's charge to all His kingdom is to "fight the good fight of the faith" (1 Tim. 6:12). It is "good" because it is right. It is a war worth fighting. It is a fight to keep the faith (2 Tim. 4:7), seize the faith (1 Tim. 6:12), and hold the faith (1 Tim. 1:19)—a gutsy struggle to maintain persevering trust in Christ.

It is a spiritual war, where the fighters wage against ideas and arguments that oppose the knowledge of God (2 Cor. 10:3-6). This knowledge is the gospel of Christ—the culminating message of all the Bible. It must be kept, seized, and held at all costs. To fail is to yield the Great Throne—your heart.

3. How would you describe the Good War in your own words? And how critical is this war to you today?

4. What are some things in your life that wage war against the knowledge of God? How do they do this? How do you respond?

5. How can you keep, seize, and hold the faith so strongly that false kings may not triumph over your heart? Are you effective in waging the Good War?

WAGING THE GOOD WAR

The Bible tells us that "we do not wrestle against flesh and blood, but against the rulers" of dark places—the false kings who hate God (Eph. 6:12). These frauds do not fight with sword and shield, but with shame and satisfaction. They use hurt and desires to lure you away from the faith.

Whatever distracts you from Christ must be fought and ultimately destroyed (2 Cor. 10:4-5). This includes apathy, laziness, indifference, comfort, luxury, weariness, fear, shame, unfaithfulness, carelessness, and every pastime and pleasure you enjoy. When these things compete with Christ, they are at that very moment your enemy, seeking to dethrone the Rightful King.

6. What are some of your favorite things to do? Have they helped you grow stronger in faith, or have they been a distraction?

7. How do you think these things distract you? What can you do to ensure they do not take the place of Christ on the Great Throne?

8. What has this lesson helped you see more clearly? Do you need to make some changes based on what you've learned? How so?

CONCLUSION

When things in your life occupy your mind, they are contending for the position that rightfully belongs to Christ. And they will win if the war is not fought. Remember, you did not decide to go to war: it was brought to you. Fight the good fight. Wage the good warfare. Keep Jesus your priority.

LESSON THREE
THE SURE CASUALTY

INDEED, ALL WHO DESIRE TO LIVE A GODLY LIFE IN CHRIST JESUS WILL BE PERSECUTED.

— 2 TIMOTHY 3:12 —

THE STORY CONTINUES

The living quarters burn like tinder. Smoke rises from the loft. The walls are bruised with ash and windows shattered. The Dark Ages have never been darker. The sun, like a breath of fresh air, breaks through the castle scars to illuminate the casualties of war. There is heartache, pain, anger, and suffering. Tragedy is all that war leaves behind.

You breathe deeply as if to catch yourself from fainting. Relieved, the cries of conflict have settled for the moment. There is just enough time to survey the devastation, possibly even rebuild some of what's been broken. But time is fleeting. The horns will soon cry out for battle yet again.

You restore only that which helps you in battle. The only spoil of war is victory and it is enough. To keep the Rightful King on the Great Throne softens the blow of agony. Casualty, no matter how severe, is worthy of the benevolent King's continued rule.

OPENING THOUGHTS

1. What are some things you would die for? What are some things you cannot do without? Why?

2. While we may not see it, the casualties of war are all around us and within us. How do you think this narrative relates to the Good War for the faith?

CASUALTY OF OUTWARD HARDSHIP

Jesus said these rather shocking words: "I have not come to bring peace but a sword" (Matt. 10:34). If that were not painstaking enough, what He said next would be the final straw to break the camel's back: "For I have come to set a man against his father, and a daughter against her mother, and a daughter-in-law against her mother-in-law" (Matt. 10:35). He was speaking of the Good War.

Jesus certainly brings peace to those He rules from the Great Throne, but that peace is only realized among those in His kingdom. He did not promise we would have peace with those who hate Him. Rather, He said those who hate Him will hate you just as much (Jn. 15:18). Living for Christ often means those who live for the world will oppose you. This is true even with friends. At some point, desires will conflict and people will get hurt.

3. Have you ever experienced opposition from the world when doing good for Christ? How did you feel? How did you overcome it?

4. Even friends can oppose you when you side with God. What has been your experience with your friends? How have they viewed your loyalty to the Rightful King?

5. What are some ways you have encouraged yourself to stay true to Jesus instead of giving in to your own desires?

CASUALTY OF INWARD SUFFERING

The "sword" that Christ brings suggests that war will exist between those "who live a godly life in Christ Jesus" and those who satisfy themselves with the ungodly desires of the world (2 Tim. 3:12). But the sting of the sharp blade is not only felt by the outward prod from our enemies. It is also felt by the inward prick of our flesh.

Loyalty to the Rightful King will mean disloyalty—even hate—to other things that contend for the Great Throne. Jesus said, "Whoever does not take his cross and follow me is not worthy of me." He said whoever desires to remain loyal to their ungodly desires will lose the Good War. But those who suffer the inward angst of denial will win the Good War, though they have lost their worldly pleasures (Matt. 10:38-39).

6. In what ways have you suffered by resisting your flesh? Has it been easy in comparison to the outward hardship from others?

7. Are there other fleshly desires and worldly comforts that distract you from your loyalty to Jesus? Why is it hard to let them go?

8. How has this lesson encouraged you to keep, seize, and hold the faith in Christ during hardship and suffering? (See how Romans 8:31–39 can help.)

CONCLUSION

When the Rightful King rules from the Great Throne, there is a lot at stake. We cannot serve two kings. We will be loyal to one and not the other, but never both. And, loyalty to one means disloyalty to the other. (The false kings hate disloyalty!) Moreover, your change in loyalty means a certain uncomfortable denial within your flesh. So the Good War is fought against the Rightful King's enemies and your inner desires that you once indulged. Don't be surprised by casualties of war (1 Pet. 4:12).

LESSON FOUR

THE SHARP SWORD

For the word of God is living and active, sharper than any two-edged sword, piercing to the division of soul and of spirit, of joints and of marrow, and discerning the thoughts and intentions of the heart.

— HEBREWS 4:12 —

THE STORY CONTINUES

———————◇———————

The Rightful King's bounteous rule satisfies the soul. It aids you in the Good War with strength and cause. But it doesn't mean that the fight is effortless. Nay, the battles seem to grow more arduous as the hours pass. Each battle proves more grueling than the last. So you refresh yourself in modest victories.

If it were not for the armor graciously given to you by the King, you would have fallen to the blows of the enemy by now. Rather, you march earnestly into battle, confidently equipped with a soldier's carapace and a warrior's weapons.

Your breastplate is impenetrable. Your helmet and shoes secure. Your waist is girded and a shield is your added defense. But it is with the sword that you slay your enemy. It is sharper than any weapon. It separates flesh from bone. Not even stone can withstand its razor! It is a soldier's kindred. He has nothing without his sword.

———————◇———————

OPENING THOUGHTS

1. If a soldier has only his armor, how is he still vulnerable in battle? Why is it important for him to have weapons of attack?

2. Does this remind you of anything in the Christian life? How does the sharp sword relate to your walk with Christ in a sinful world?

A WEAPON OF DEFENSE

Spiritual war requires spiritual weapons. The Bible tells us that the Good War is a "stand against the schemes of the devil." It is not a fight against "flesh and blood, but against rulers, against authorities, against the cosmic powers over this present darkness, against the spiritual force of evil in the heavenly places" (Eph. 6:11–12).

To slay the enemy, God gives us "the sword of the spirit, which is the word of God" (Eph. 6:17). Scripture is the perfect weapon. Even Christ wielded it when faced with the schemes of the devil (Matt. 4:4–10). He deflected Satan's attack with precision, making use of exact scriptures to contradict the deception. Jesus was trained to swing His sword—trained to understand the Scripture. Satan's words were no match.

3. The "schemes of the devil" refer to Satan's deceitful methods. How does the "sword of the Spirit" help us against these schemes?

4. How important is it for you to know and understand God's Word? What happens to the Christian soldier who is not trained in the sword of the Spirit?

5. Has the Word of God been useful in your combat against temptation? In what ways has it helped you deflect the enemy's fiery darts?

A WEAPON OF OFFENSE

The sword of the Spirit is also a powerful offensive weapon. It is capable of inflicting fatal blows to the enemy. "For the word of God is living and active, sharper than any two-edged sword, piercing to the division of soul and spirit, of joints and marrow, and discerning the thoughts and intentions of the heart" (Heb. 4:12).

Scripture is so sharp it severs the complex arguments against God. Nothing is more powerful. Nothing is more authoritative. Nothing is more suitable in the hands of a soldier battling in the Good War.

6. What do you suppose is meant when describing the Word of God as living, active, sharp, piercing, and discerning?

7. What makes the Bible stand out and above all other books? Why is it so important for your battle against sin?

8. In your honest assessment, do you think that you are well-equipped for the Good War? What sort of things can you do to become better with the sword?

CONCLUSION

As defender of the Great Throne, you must divert the attacks of the enemy and cut his deceptive darts to pieces. It is not enough to withstand him in battle. You must go on the offense and slay him so that his attack ends.

A soldier cannot battle without his sword. He is unable to stop his enemy. For this reason, the Christian soldier must know his sword assuredly and swing it with precision. He cannot wave it around haphazardly, but with intention and determination. Know the Word. Swing the sword!

LESSON FIVE

THE STRONG SHIELD

In all circumstances take
up the shield of faith,
with which you can
extinguish all the flaming
darts of the evil one.

— EPHESIANS 6:16 —

THE STORY CONTINUES

The horns blast yet again. Another wave of battle commences. Arcs of flaming arrows illuminate the dark clouds of a ruined land coughing up the midnight smoke. A cry from your fellow soldiers announces the incoming darts!

One hand holds the sword ever so tightly. The other flings the metallic shield to block the intense light. Securing yourself to the rock beneath, you hear the blazing arrows whistle by and sink into the ground. The fire is so close you hear it crackle.

Your shield protects you. It is dark beneath its guard, but the clanging noise of fiery darts ricocheting remind you that it's better to be hidden in its shade. So you sit tight and endure the noise, the heat, and the unknown.

OPENING THOUGHTS

1. In ancient times, wooden shields were plated with metal, covered with leather, and saturated with water so that they would not only deflect arrows, but extinguish their flame. Why do you think this was important in battle?

2. Does this illustration remind you of anything in your spiritual life? How might a shield be useful when temptations are thrown upon you?

TRUST IN A POWERFUL GOD

All people live by some form of faith. Each time we sit in a chair, we trust it will hold us up. When we eat food, we trust it is not poisoned. We put our trust in airplanes and automobiles, confident they will keep us safe. Faith makes life as we know it possible. But faith in God is far more reliable and more important than everyday faith.

Faith is only as reliable as the trustworthiness of its object. Since Jesus is far more powerful and dependable than anything on earth, He is most reliable in our life. Christian faith never fails because Jesus never fails. This is why God tells us to "take up the shield of faith, with which you can extinguish the flaming darts of the evil one" and to do so "in all circumstances" (Eph. 6:16).

3. In what ways is everyday faith different from Christian faith? In what ways, if any, are they similar?

4. How do you suppose the "shield of faith" can extinguish the "flaming darts of the evil one"? Give examples of how this happens in your personal life.

5. How has faith in Jesus helped you through troublesome times? How would these times have turned out if you did not have faith in God?

TRUST IN A PROVEN GOD

The Bible teaches us that faith is trusting that God is who He says He is and will do what He says (Heb. 11:6). It is saying with our heart, "I will follow Jesus no matter my circumstances and expectations." It is to believe God and obey Him. The opposite, which is sin, is to believe Satan and to follow him.

Taking up the shield of faith could be seen as holding on to what God has told us in Scripture, and trusting that He will keep His Word, even when it looks impossible to us. A proverb tells us, "Every word of God proves true; he is a shield to those who take refuge in him" (Prov. 30:5).

6. What do you remember about the fall of Adam and Eve (Genesis 3:1–7)? What does this teach us about faith in God and the "flaming darts of the evil one"?

7. Why is it important that God's Word is proven true—without error? How does it help you in your faith? How does it strengthen your shield?

8. As you consider your life, have you trusted God in all circumstances? How can you be more confident in God's promises in the days to come?

CONCLUSION

The Bible reminds us that being born of God is being an overcomer of the enemy's tactics and ways of the world. "This is the victory that has overcome the world—our faith" (1 Jn. 5:4). When the Rightful King rules from the Great Throne, He rules with unbeatable power, and He carries you through impossible battles. In the end, those who fight for Him will be triumphant; for He is the shield that protects us from the evil one. Believe God and have faith in Him.

LESSON SIX

THE TRUSTY CLAN

IF ONE MEMBER SUFFERS, ALL
SUFFER TOGETHER; IF ONE
MEMBER IS HONORED, ALL
REJOICE TOGETHER.

— 1 CORINTHIANS 12:26 —

THE STORY CONTINUES

The battles wage without end. You toil and strive with sword and shield, but the enemy is persistent, unwilling to surrender. So determined is the evil one that you wonder if victory is practical. It would seem not.

You are tired and weak. The weight of your armor is heavier than when it first rested on you. Your sword, although as sharp as its first swing, is leaden. Your shield, still resistant and firm, is drug along the earth's floor. Sweat has soaked your clothing, and blood has stained your skin.

In mind, you are resilient and resolute. You call yourself to stand upright and charge forward, but your body struggles to respond. It cannot go much longer. It needs rest. So it falls to one knee and shocks the lungs to breath more deeply.

The enemy, seeing your weariness, lunges forward to plunge a fatal blow. His dagger moves so swiftly it separates ash from flame. It is certain to pierce. Then suddenly, a familiar sword swings before you and slays the enemy! A strong arm grabs you by your side and lifts you up. You are surrounded by your trusty clan.

OPENING THOUGHTS

1. How important is a soldier's fellow in battle? What advantage does a warrior have when he is accompanied by other warriors?

2. How does this illustrate your life? Do you see the value of other Christians joining you in a fight against temptation? How so?

ONE BODY, MANY PARTS

The Bible describes the church as a body. It is a living network of people who belong to Christ and are ruled by His Word, which tells us God specifically formed and arranged the body to perform certain functions. Like your body, there are certain parts that do the seeing, the hearing, the walking, lifting, and so forth. Each has an important role in the life as a whole.

When one part of the body is weak, God uses the other parts to help so that all parts "may have the same care for one another" (1 Cor. 12:24-25). It's an "all-in-together" work, with each part working with and for the other parts to maintain strength against the evil one (1 Thess. 5:11). "If one member suffers, all suffer together; if one member is honored, all rejoice together" (1 Cor. 12:26).

3. What are the advantages of belonging to a church of "all-in-together" people? What are the disadvantages when you do not?

4. What does it mean for you when considering the church as one body with many parts? How important are you to the body?

5. How do you think we, as a church, can suffer and rejoice together? What does this mean in your life right now?

MANY PARTS, ONE WORK

Your hand can never tell your arm that it is going somewhere else. Rather, where the arm goes, the hand goes. If your hand were to leave your arm, it would no longer work. The body labors as one.

Since the body of Christ—the church—is to glorify God, the body must live Christ-like. It should prioritize the gospel and slay sin when it sneaks in (Eph. 4:25). To do so, we need each other. We need to encourage, defend, and rebuke each other if we are to win this Great War on sin (Gal. 6:1).

6. How can we all glorify God together as one work? Practically speaking, describe how it would look in today's world.

7. A proverb says that "Iron sharpens iron, and one man sharpens another" (Prov. 27:17). What do you suppose this means? How does it relate to this lesson?

8. How have you grown more appreciative of your church? What actions and attitudes do you need to change in order to benefit from this "one" body?

CONCLUSION

Going to war alone will never work. You need your fellow soldiers with you. And they need you. The Bible tells us to "bear one another's burdens, and so fulfill the law of Christ" (Gal. 6:2). When one of us needs care, we should come to aid. When one of us needs strength, we should come to hold up. And when one is falling to temptation, we should come to restore in a spirit of gentleness. Our Lord has given us our armor. He has also given us each other. Be grateful that you are not alone in the fight.

CLOSING

THE FINAL VICTORY

"I AM THE ALPHA AND THE
OMEGA," SAYS THE LORD GOD,
"WHO IS AND WHO WAS AND
WHO IS TO COME, THE
ALMIGHTY."

— REVELATION 1:8 —

THE STORY CONTINUES

As the noise of battle resonates loudest and the agony of war hurts most deeply, the Rightful King rises from the Great Throne. His feet thunder and quake the ground beneath you. His feet thump a wide span from step to step. This is no ordinary walk. He is coming to wage war.

Those in the arena of war stand still. Even the evil ones cease their bloodshed. Swords no longer swing. Bows lay down their arrows. Sword and shield repose on the ground. No one speaks. Only the breath of the King can be heard. His inhale and exhale sounds like wind moving throughout the blood-stained fields.

His steps become louder as He makes His way to the castle entrance. The hordes of sin shake with terror. The soldiers of the King are infused with strength. With each booming footstep, emotions spike. Then, the doors swing open and He speaks.

"I AM THE ALPHA AND THE OMEGA, WHO IS AND WHO WAS AND WHO IS TO COME, THE ALMIGHTY."

It is like nothing ever spoken before. His voice, like a double-edged sword, sweeps across the fields of battle and all who sought the Great Throne are flung to their death. It is the end of the Good War!

And so a future time will come. Until then, unite with your trusty clan, take up sword and shield, and wage the good warfare on all who seek the Great Throne which rightfully belongs to God. For in the end, He will rise and slay the enemy once and for all, and reward those who kept the Great Throne defended.

NOTES AND GUIDES

The lessons were designed to guide the reader without additional resources. However, leaders might find the aids below helpful in guiding discussions and provoking deeper contemplation.

LESSON ONE: THE GREAT THRONE

Before anything else, the student must see Jesus as the King of his heart. Nothing else in the guide will make any sense if this is not true. So, in this lesson we present the gospel and call the student to repentance by surrendering the throne of his heart to Christ. Jesus needs to be our conquering King and rule if our lives are to be whole. Only He can give us a new heart with new love and loyalty.

Here are some scriptures and quote to consider:

- **Proverbs 3:5** — Trust in the LORD with all your heart, and do not lean on your own understanding.

- **Ephesians 2:1-3** — And you were dead in the trespasses and sins in which you once walked, following the course of this world, following the prince of the power of the air, the spirit that is now at work in the sons of disobedience—among whom we all once lived in the passions of our flesh, carrying out the desires of the body and the mind, and were by nature children of wrath, like the rest of mankind.

- **A.W. Tozer** — The neglected heart will soon be a heart overrun with worldly thoughts; the neglected life will soon become a moral chaos.

LESSON TWO: THE GOOD WAR

Many things in this world fight for our thoughts trying to stir our affections away from Christ. But, our thoughts belong to Him. If we do not carefully and forcefully wage war against those worldly whims, they will win and take our thoughts captive. In this lesson, we learn to prioritize Jesus and His gospel in order to wage the good warfare against the attacks of the world.

Here are some scriptures and quote to consider:

- **1 Timothy 6:12** — Fight the good fight of the faith. Take hold of the eternal life to which you were called and about which you made the good confession in the presence of many witnesses.

- **2 Corinthians 10:3-6** — For though we walk in the flesh, we are not waging war according to the flesh. For the weapons of our warfare are not of the flesh but have divine power to destroy strongholds. We destroy arguments and every lofty opinion raised against the knowledge of God, and take every thought captive to obey Christ, being ready to punish every disobedience, when your obedience is complete.

- **Charles Spurgeon** — A war against falsehood, a war against sin, is God's war; it is a war which commends itself to every Christian man, seeing he is quite certain that he has the seal of God's approval when he goes to wage war against God's enemies. Beloved, we have no doubt whatever, when we lift up our voices like a trumpet against sin, that our warfare is justified by the eternal laws of justice.

LESSON THREE: THE SURE CASUALTY

Life, particularly life as a Christian, is full of troubles. The world does not surrender easily, nor does it leave without a fight. Wounds are inevitable. And, the first thing to be wounded is our flesh, which stirs up trouble when we wage our war against temptation. In this lesson, we discuss the casualties of war—the grumbling old self.

Here are some scriptures and quote to consider:

- **John 15:18** — If the world hates you, know that it has hated me before it hated you. If you were of the world, the world would love you as its own; but because you are not of the world, but I chose you out of the world, therefore the world hates you.

- **Romans 8:31, 35-39** — What then shall we say to these things? If God is for us, who can be against us? Who shall separate us from the love of Christ? Shall tribulation, or distress, or persecution, or famine, or nakedness, or danger, or sword? As it is written, "For your sake we are being killed all the day long; we are regarded as sheep to be slaughtered." No, in all these things we are more than conquerors through him who loved us. For I am sure that neither death nor life, nor angels nor rulers, nor things present nor things to come, nor powers, nor height nor depth, nor anything else in all creation, will be able to separate us from the love of God in Christ Jesus our Lord. indeed is interceding for us. Who shall separate us from the love of Christ? Shall tribulation, or distress, or persecution, or famine, or nakedness, or danger, or sword?

- **Tim Keller** — Suffering is actually at the heart of the Christian story ... The best people often have terrible lives. Job is one example, and Jesus—the ultimate 'Job,' the only truly, fully innocent sufferer—is another.

LESSON FOUR: THE SHARP SWORD

The weapons of war are critical to our victory. As Christians, we need to learn the importance of God's Word. It is our sharp sword in the battle waged against sin. Wielding it correctly matters. In this lesson, we draw our attention to the importance of reading and meditating on God's Word.

Here are some scriptures and quote to consider:

- **Ephesians 6:11-12** — Put on the whole armor of God, that you may be able to stand against the schemes of the devil. For we do not wrestle against flesh and blood, but against the rulers, against the authorities, against the cosmic powers over this present darkness, against the spiritual forces of evil in the heavenly places.

- **Ephesians 6:17** — Take the sword of the Spirit, which is the word of God, praying at all times in the Spirit, with all prayer and supplication. To that end, keep alert with all perseverance, making supplication for all the saints, and also for me, that words may be given to me in opening my mouth boldly to proclaim the mystery of the gospel, for which I am an ambassador in chains, that I may declare it boldly, as I ought to speak.

- **Charles Spurgeon** — The Captain's voice is clear as a trumpet. Take the sword! No Christian man here will have been obedient to our text unless with clear, sharp, and decisive firmness, courage, and resolve, he takes the sword.

LESSON FIVE: THE STRONG SHIELD

Alongside the sword (God's Word) is the strong shield. It is also critical to winning in the battle against sin. The shield of faith helps us by casting our burdens on God and being confident in His power. The shield protects us from distrust, and assures our triumphant end. In this lesson, we turn our attention to the faith we must have as Christians in the life of war.

Here are some scriptures and quote to consider:

- **Ephesians 6:16** — In all circumstances take up the shield of faith, with which you can extinguish all the flaming darts of the evil one.

- **1 Corinthians 10:13** — No temptation has overtaken you that is not common to man. God is faithful, and he will not let you be tempted beyond your ability, but with the temptation he will also provide the way of escape, that you may be able to endure it.

- **Hebrews 11:6** — And without faith it is impossible to please him, for whoever would draw near to God must believe that he exists and that he rewards those who seek him.

- **Charles Spurgeon** — Then when the enemy makes his cut at the sword-arm of a Christian, to disable him, if possible, from future service, faith protects the arm like a shield, and he is able to do exploits for his Master, and go forth, still conquering, and to conquer, in the name of Him who has loved us.

LESSON SIX: THE TRUSTY CLAN

In the final lesson, we learn that our local church and Christian friends are huge help in this life. They are like our fellow soldiers who bear arms with us in battle. They hold us up in prayer and hold us accountable in love. They bring us strength and walk with us. In addition to the full armor of God, we are granted each other. So, we are never alone in the fight.

Here are some scriptures and quote to consider:

- **1 Thessalonians 5:11** — Therefore encourage one another and build one another up, just as you are doing.

- **Ephesians 4:25** — Therefore, having put away falsehood, let each one of you speak the truth with his neighbor, for we are members one of another.

- **Matthew Henry** — Most men are dead in their sins, and therefore have no sight or sense of the spiritual burden of sin. Feeling the weight and burden of our sins, we must seek to be eased thereof by the Savior, and be warned against every sin.

FROM THE AUTHOR
JACOB ABSHIRE

Hi. My name is Jacob Abshire and I am desperate for Jesus Christ. He is my way, truth, and life. My wife agrees—for herself, that is. She is equally desperate. Together, we love to call Him ours.

We also love to raise our four children to call on Jesus the same way. We live in Houston—the greatest "country" in the United States. We love to worship with our spiritual family at Northeast Houston Baptist Church.

My joy in life is to use creative means to bring others closer to God's word in order to find the riches of God's truth for the glory of God's son. In other words, I am "creatively making disciples." One of the ways I do this is by writing. First, I write at my personal blog (jacobabshire.com) where I turn up writings about church and family life, ministry, leadership, technology, scripture, and general musings. Second, I write books (because my friends pressure me to). In 2009, I published *Forgiveness: A Commentary on Philemon*. Three years later, I followed it up with *Faith: A Commentary on James*. Both are part of an ongoing series I call, "Reader's Commentaries," because they are comprehensive commentaries in a readable form. (One reader said that they are for people who hate to read but want to learn the Bible.) I also write small group discussion guides and design artwork consistent with my joy (all of which are available on my site).

For more information, visit my blog. If you have questions, shoot me a message on my contact page. I usually respond the same day. Grace and peace.

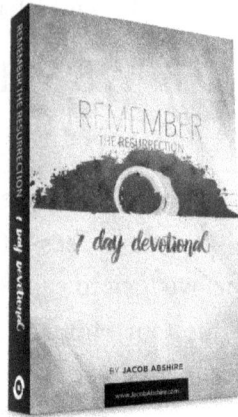

REMEMBER THE RESURRECTION

7 DAY DEVOTIONAL

How often do you remember the resurrection? After Jesus was crucified, His disciples were deeply troubled. They were saddened by His death. This is where we begin our devotional journey. We will ask ourselves as the angels asked Mary, "Why are you weeping?"

Then, we will follow along the story looking for more questions and inquiring them of ourselves, thinking more deeply about the resurrection and what it means for us today. We will join the disciples and seek in wonder, see in amazement, savor in understanding, satisfy in assurance, surrender in reverence, and finally, share in excitement.

Together, with the Holy Scriptures, we will go back in time, walk with the disciples, and personally reflect on the importance of the resurrection. My aim in this devotional series is to help you become more mindful of the resurrection through life lessons on faith.

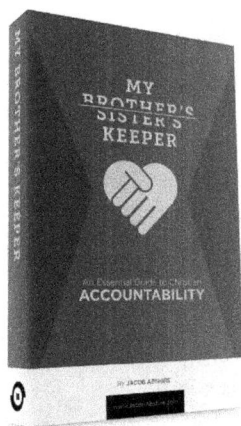

MY BROTHER'S KEEPER

AN ESSENTIAL GUIDE TO
CHRISTIAN ACCOUNTABILITY

"Fortify your friends to mortify your sins." Stephen the Levite was right on target with those words. God tells us to "put to death what is earthly in you" (Col. 3:5). He says, "For if you live according to the flesh you will die, but if by the Spirit you put to death the deeds of the body, you will live" (Rom. 8:13).

Killing sin is not only a command, but a characteristic of the Christian. If we are "of Christ," we follow His Spirit, not the sinful world. Still, putting off the flesh and putting on Christ (Rom. 13:14) is not always easy alone. For this reason, God gave us each other. He gave us Christian accountability.

In *My Brother's Keeper: An Essential Guide to Christian Accountability*, I discuss the concept of teaming up to kill sin and practical ways to thrive in it. From meeting to mediating, this book provides the tools you need to fortify your friends and mortify your sins.

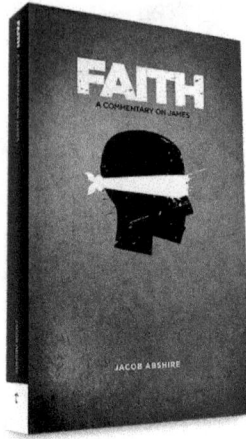

FAITH

A COMMENTARY ON JAMES

Do your troubles reveal faith that can save? In the Bible, James progresses through a series of troubles like the ones you face and ones you may not even know you face. He calls them trials. When our sinful lives collide against the holiness of God and our pride is smashed to pieces, we find the foremost gift of God as deposited in us by Christ. In our wreckage, we can learn to appreciate our troubles for what they are—divinely purposed trials that reveal and mature our belief in Christ. In this book, we will follow along with James and see what we can uncover about the foremost gift of God: Faith.

Find out why trials are our greatest gifts ... This book explores 18 characteristics of faith in order to help you mature as a Christ follower. But before you can begin your journey, you must be ready and willing to let the waves wreck you again and again.

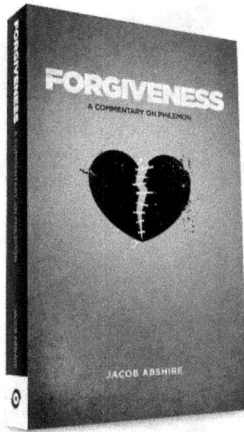

FORGIVENESS

A COMMENTARY ON PHILEMON

Despite its small size, the book of Philemon is quite colossal, theologically speaking. It instructs us on forgiveness and does so in a unique and practical way. And while it does this, it gently teaches on matters of equality, fellowship, edification and more. Only 25 verses long, it packs 25 chapters worth of divine guidance for us all.

In this book, we will unpack these divinities so that we can think and behave more like our Lord, who is a forgiving God (Ex. 34:6-7). Technically, this book is called a "commentary" on Philemon; however, it has been written in a way that is unlike typical commentaries, which often read like textbooks, focus on individual passages, and have a choppy flow. The flow of this book is fluid, transitioning from point to point, like topical books do. However, in this book all of the points are posited by scripture. This is a commentary for those who don't like commentaries.

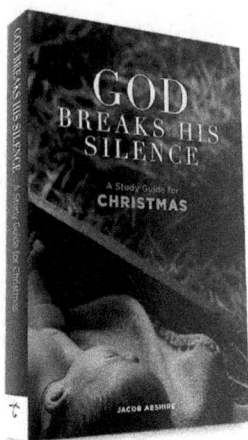

GOD BREAKS HIS SILENCE

A STUDY GUIDE FOR CHRISTMAS

It has become easier each year to forget what the Christmas season is all about. There's the hustle in buying, the traffic in the streets, and that irritated lady who mouths off to the store clerk when they run out of Elmos. So many things can distract us from—pardon the cliché—the reason for the season.

If we can prepare ourselves ahead, this time of the year can be wonderfully useful to our families. We have to be intentional. We have to take advantage of the sights, sounds, and smells, and use them to stir our affections toward heaven.

This short study guide is aimed at doing just that. It focuses on two different stories about two different people from two different cities who respond two different ways to one similar message—salvation is coming.

For more resources like this visit:
JacobAbshire.com